There is a wonderful sense of presence in the poetry
of Juliet Carpenter. A sense by which the ordinary is
embodied and allowed its natural radiance - the illness,
the birdsong, the long curled forefinger. Her work is
incarnation, an opportunity to be reminded and to
re-member.

     Neil McKinlay
     Somatic Dharma Teacher

It is a joyous privilege to read Julie Carpenter's very
powerful and extremely perceptive poetry.

     Ronald Billingsley,
     Associate Professor Emeritus,
     University of Colorado, Boulder

At the close of Julie Carpenter's storied career as a family
physician in and around Boulder, Colorado, she opens
this book of her poetry to us. Not surprisingly, we find
intimate and honest anatomies of moments given into,
painful and pleasurable and simply here in their passing
uniqueness, both "brittle and light." We see through the
doctor's eye into her heart.

     Reed Bye
     Naropa University

WHERE
A
PIECE
OF ME
IS
TORN AWAY

"Memento" and "Give" were both published in THE HUMAN TOUCH, Volume 7, 2014, which is the poetry, prose, and visual art journal published annually by the University of Colorado Anschutz Medical Campus.

"Before the Flood" was published in 2017 in UNDER THE DEVIL'S THUMB by the Sockwood Press, a literary anthology of work by writers and artists from Blackhawk to Allenspark, Colorado.

Three of the Haiku from the poem "In the Shrineroom" were published in the BHAVANA SOCIETY MAGAZINE, in November 2001.

An earlier version of "Millie" was published in May 2002 in THE JOURNAL OF PALLIATIVE CARE, Leeds, England.

All photographs, throughout the book and on the cover, were taken by the author.

This book is set in Goudy Old Style and Sabon MT.
Book design by Laura Marshall.

WHERE A PIECE OF ME IS TORN AWAY
© Juliet Carpenter 2020

ISBN 978-1-887997-41-6

BB BAKSUN BOOKS & ARTS

WHERE A PIECE
OF ME
IS
TORN AWAY

POEMS BY
JULIET CARPENTER

BABoB

BAKSUN BOOKS & ARTS

TABLE OF CONTENTS

Distance Between Us

What is Left

Please call me by my true names
so I can wake up
and the door of my heart
could be left open

Thich Nhat Hanh

These poems come from the wellspring of the life
I have been so blessed to be living. These poems arose
from 43 years as a practicing physician, a life raising
two amazing young men, loving friends and family, and
a deep bond with nature. The opportunity of sharing
deeply the journeys of their lives with patients and
friends, through birth, illness, joy, loss and death, has
brought me incredible riches.

Many of these poems appeared almost complete
from the ether, in dreams, hiking, or after days of sitting.
Others required hours of honing, editing, and rereading.
I offer them as gifts to you.

LEANING EVEN CLOSER

VOTING DAY

a physician remembers

I place my purple hat, gray gloves on the table
You   ask my name   address

It is cold out   snowing
You   sit stiffly
Tables piled with brownies, chocolate chip cookies, shortbread

What lies between us
he would be twenty three or four   grown   a man

I hesitate
Our lowered eyes
we suffocated
Far away our hearts were shrinkwrapped

You place the ballot in my hand
A number which is mine
between us   he is always less than one day old

I tear the stub
the son you never held
the pain that never leaves

I place my ballot in the box
we have forgiven

MEMENTO

I am not sure
how long
it was since she
inhabited this body
or how long she had been gone
I only know
that bullet
into her occipital lobe
through the mouth
dislodged something

she woke up
white sheets
ICU
expecting to be dead
the usual faces
were all there
her arm and leg
not working

last night I saw the moon rise
a muted orange
in a shower of stars

seventeen years
no one can tell
except
right thumb and forefinger
permanently curled
memory carried
      there

MILLIE

I am kneeling beside her bed
I am leaning over close to her head

I am yelling into ears that don't hear
She says *I want my glasses is it Saturday*

I am feeling the swelling in her feet
I am smelling her breath

She says *people don't like me nobody comes*
I say *your parakeets are singing*

people don't like me   eyes filling
I am listening to her tears her belly her lungs

Gnarled hands clench mine
I am leaning over now even closer

We are embracing
She is kissing my hands I am leaving

I am listening to her heart

Apostrophe

Below the waist
the cancer has taken

over
above

it's like any other
day

if she knows
what's happening

below she is not
letting on

another KOOL
another Irish

whiskey
why quit

now
that it's

she does not
does not

say the word
over   ever

pretend
just one more day

her brother he died
a horrible death
ten months of dying
its eaten her away
does she feel my shudder

when I can't see
where the rectum ends
her vagina somehow missing

nothing left
I'm the doctor
I'm supposed to

examine her
say something

helpful
Say it's not as

bad as
dying

her eyes ever question
I'm supposed to

say
it's not
so bad

arrange
bed sheets

make sense
I'm supposed

to be
hopeful

The Haunting

She called
sometime between 2 and 4 am

When she awoke one by one
lights went on until she was drowned in it
then she called

They were outside
at the door
knocking
pulling the window bells
making the wind chimes blurt
atonal messages she did not want to hear

She called him then
every Wednesday
pulling him from deep sleep
there was no one else to call

He managed to listen
place a reassuring word
into her consciousness
help her through till morning

Crucify demons
No   only tame them for this night

ICU

On the monitor
your heartbeats tick across the screen so fast
you already so tenuous
the racket of the metal fan
drowns out all but the loudest beeps

you motionless
clear, black, red, white, yellow wires
tether you to your bed
to life

you speak in a whisper
please stay
touch me
tell me
I'm not dying

hours later
you ask me
remove your hand
a lifeline
no longer

giving permission
to let go

Too good for her

She grew into her cancer
as if it were another
costume
it took over
the right side of her neck.
Her slight body
a pendulum

Peacock feathers
lace the finest silk
diamonds and moonstone
were not too good
for her

it was
the uncertainty
and gracelessness
of leaving that troubled her
left her groundless
a limousine would
have been better

CLOUDLESS

he heard his freedom calling
and calling
put on your walking boots
tonight it is time

always you have walked the edges
full circle
the enchanted path
lined lavender
stone after stone underfoot

stars beckon
brighter than suns
the way is swift
in an instant
bodies frozen

the silken thread is loosed
from the crimson kite
souls flung into the heavens
embracing what we do not know

unanchored
we gather threads
join the stars

you go
not where we thought you were going
but beyond

Burnout

fifty years

this life

a well

water drawn

out

and up

into

their mouths

open bodies

under   skin

trying to hide

my own closet

empty

ELEGY

In memory of Justin 1982-1992

Walk softly gentle brother
tread lightly till we meet
the stars which danced around your head
now twinkle at your feet

You've shed the coat that once you wore
returned it to the earth
and now you journey towards the home
you knew before your birth

Surround yourself with rings of light
the road it may be long
and gird yourself with Father's love
and Mother's tender song

The staff of life is passed once more
with pain for us today
and yet   dear one   you are released
to go upon your way

IN REVERENCE

Ghost Bear

it was the carcass of a baby bear
all downy soft and brown
splayed flat in the bottom of their gully
fur and claws on tiny feet
a few bones
all that remain

further on
pelt of coyote
bushy tail

I know we come to this place
hidden in the dark bottom
to make a refuge
sound of our world grown distant
in uncanny quiet

far down the trail
next to the creek
where our voices echo
loudspeakers

I am skittish
invading this sanctuary
canyon of cougar, bear, coyote
this place   eerily inhuman
wild ghosts palpable

THE THUNDER THEIR WINGS

Clouds of rosy finch dive
inebriated with morning
and two feet of snow
whirl and spiral

inebriated with morning
they make their own wind
whirl and spiral
falling over each other in sunshine

they make their own wind
chant in high register
falling over each other in sunshine
leap skyward in unison

chant in high register
and two feet of snow
leap skyward in unison
Clouds of rosy finch dive

SHOULDER SEASON

The road undulates
unfurling out of winter

Remains of melting snow
and new mud inspire
spikes of tawny grasses
kinnikinnick
the first spring beauties

The road stretching its limbs
in pastel sunlight
fades away into yellow

Where do they go

Sunlight
snow that glitters
as it sinks
squandering its prisms
to water

BEFORE THE FLOOD

i am sure there have been days
like this one
thunder throbbing
a dark afternoon
lit by daggers of light
my sturdy a-frame shaking
on its concrete foundation

this storm
bombards my land
relentless
torrents
the path to the back meadow
turned into a river of mud

i watch the slashing rain
two inches in one hour
suddenly
clouds separate
five minutes of sun
before cumuli retake the sky

night falls
rain falls
rain falls and falls
i put pails under spots where the roof leaks
i go to bed

listen to the clatter
as if this rainfall was like any other

an ordinary lullaby
begging sleep
and i sleep
reassured by the sound
of thirsty earth drinking
dead to the deluge to come

OWL

last night i saw you fly
out of darkness
plunging into moonlight

you the only thing
moving

into the pines
i watch
great white wings beating

and when

you are gone
like a phantom

the space
in the night

where you were

STRETCHING OUT

PRAGUE: PRISONER

In the palace with a thousand rooms
she could walk forever
red hair streaming behind her
what is light like
through pink windows
ceilings as high as the sky
great columns and brass angels at her flanks

In pale green and golden gossamer
idleness plays like a grand piano
smoothing over centuries
salon to parlor parlor to bedchamber
hallways arching her Tuesday

If only for a footprint
small heels on red carpet
lace in her chamber
organdy on her brow
whisper wistful glances
the city far below

PRAGUE: IN ST. VITUS CATHEDRAL

Snakes are anchored
in a sea of blue
red glass wraps
a heart in prison

If i lived here
i would eat the swords
which stake them to doors
i would throw stars
red and white
wield lightning
and tame flames

For the food of the violin is fire
the food of my song
the single livid eye
that bores dangerously close
to my river

PRAGUE: GIVE

If I walk down Na Prikope
I see your hand
just beyond where it is I can reach

just so far do I bend and give
enough
just to satisfy
something unseen
and I think there will be
time and time enough
to walk back and back
and give again

give up whatever I have
in my pocket to give
and place into the fingerless hand
the currency of accelerated time
before I am reaching

what I want to see is the unseen
and on the street corner
I have not given enough
to your paralyzed right side
and when my heart is already unseen
I have not broken my pride enough
to give you
my hand

PRAGUE: FESTIVAL IN THREE COLORS

for Pavel Sporcl

Voice of velvet
charms three rings
pirate soft

over verdant hills
voluptuous
honeysuckle in shadow

the cadence of laughter
in your violin
does not linger

an arpeggio

a waterfall

a lullaby

Shhh
Shhh

TIBET: OUT TO THE PLATEAU

there is a world here
valleys and sheer cliffs
etched in oyster and ash
rivers of white crystal
a man carrying a basket
of creamy cotton
balanced on his head

granite prehistoric
in white and gray
the black place glitters
when the wind howls
paint drips frozen off peaks

they camped above
where ground was flat
where they could look
over the precipice
out to the plateau

TIBET: THE MO

A fur lined coat
settles a tangle of blankets
his amma to cradle him
in the cold room
a concrete floor
no matter the bed is plywood
foam mattress soiled
his head matted with blood

before long
there is enough
hot water
for washing
right leg twisted
he does not move without anguish

we don't want to keep him
he is too sick
arriving
homemade stretcher
unconscious
but monks throw a mo
say he stays
we have no choice

TIBET: SAY YOU ARE

say you are summer rain
walking through afternoon
say you are a temple
she is alive
summer after summer walking
say you are walking over rain
alive after swelling
alive after eclipse
say you are rain
summer eclipse
after rain

say you are summer
walking temple
she over afternoon
after eclipse
after swelling
after rain
say you are
again summer
again rain
again you say
say you are summer
say you are
say you are she

Tibet: Such a Place as This

Lush green underfoot
marshy soft
I sink into mud
ruined temple walls are alive
here on this hilltop
overgrown
headache flower
larkspur gentian

Above the mountain
pushes higher
eclipsing remains
what once was a window
never asking forgiveness
nor giving a second thought
to what is gone

    I sit
      meditate
in the crumpled archway

by morning
it rains again
a slow drizzle
indoors a steamy curtain
envelopes windows

    this
the morning's weeping

TIBET: FESTIVAL

scent of coal burning
the monk's dancing is over
drunk from the cup in the sky
walking rocks under a rainbow
the moon has forgotten her setting
over the mountain that watches

in a flex of muscles and crumpled tattoo
minstrel's moccasins turn dirt
into red summer sleeves
whirling bells in a chant
turquoise
coral

imagine the glance of a child in the dark
eyes wide open

TIBET: SHATTERED

The eyes of night fall into the river
a bridge that isn't there
we slide into oblivion
concrete
where water would go

shattered glass
blood open wounds
delirium of arms and legs
purple around the eyes of night
the eyes of the witch
who always hunts before dawn

we were watched as we hurtled forward
hit hard
something
I heard
broken tumbled
upside down flailing

I just heard cries
  voices screaming.
    it was I choking out of the darkness
      calling his name
        calling his name
          calling his name

Tibet: Tourist

Black jeeps
shiny in drizzle
packed to the hilt
tripods   ropes
cameras   binoculars
telescopes in leather casings
lanky
tight
bodies in boots
raingear with too many pockets

Photographers I ask
no   birdwatchers
he growls

Brits encased in cocoons
like so many tourists
knowing where they come from
but not where they have been

NICARAGUA: EGRET

you glide
in slow motion
on the surface of the lake
determined unperturbed
your motion elegant
in shadows of dawn

mesmerized
we stare
at your beauty
your bearing
your ageless presence

across shallows
at the edge of the beach dawn throws her
blue and gold
on throbbing water

INDIA: ON THE TRAIN TO KOLKATA

piles of hay
landscape of endless fields
5:30 am
workers already toil

stacking mounds of hay into sacks
then onto
their backs

generations work together
surrounded by goats
cows chickens pond herons

in stifling heat

children make bricks from mud

tiny hands fashion good bricks

the earth swallows our tears

INDIA: TRAFFIC BALLET

we fall into the flow
veering in and out
endless motion
no spaces
cars   vans   scooters   buses
tuk-tuks   rickshaws
cows and goats
dogs   lorries   pedestrians   bicycles
taxis   motorcycles
all moving
in complex gyration

we are all in motion
swept
as if on a conveyor belt
once the motorcyclist is on our right
then in front of us

horns beep
as if speaking

all this spontaneous movement
an orchestrated
choreographed improvisation

we move seamlessly in and out
flow undaunted
one with the dance

Distance Between Us

CHARMED

You keep looking steadily my way
softness steals between us
You move to take my arm

Your face
Your eyes
sizzling green intense
penetrate the distance between us

Let me look at you all night
illuminated
my hands open
never knowing your skin

I was not ready for you
I did not anticipate you would appear
I did not know I would know you

For who you are

RECOGNITION

she lay draped across him

a swath of cloth over a sofa

it seemed that the wind

raging around them

would tear her off

peel her away

from his soft skin

they clung together somehow

held by invisible cords

then   she looked into

his vacant eyes

pulled away

INVISIBLE GIFTS

I

You have left an ice pack
and your tan wind jacket
a copy of Dave Van Ronk's autobiography
you read to me at night
an empty jar, your blue bowl
half eaten chard and kefir
a pair of olive green socks
poems of Kabir and Hafiz
your Martin Simpson and Tony McManus CDs

I wake at dawn
bring you Coleman Barks reading Rumi
Miles Davis Sketches of Spain
Jack Gilbert, Rod Stewart crooning classics
my thin childhood pillow
in navy case
now sleeps to the south
the blue side of your bed
by your oversized dresser
there a book Mary Oliver
we read to each other at night

I place these things except the pillow
of course, on your glass table
we exchange spices, tea, mushrooms
a kiss under a rainbow
at the trailhead to Finch Lake

I wake at dawn
wind gusts, joists creaking
I have no appetite for food
living on light
I don't know what's mine anymore

II

First snow dots the peaks
late autumn
I return your CDs, the kefir jar
your tan jacket and ice pack
the unfinished book
one by one I place these things
on your glass table

You return
Rumi, Mary, Kabir, Jack, Rod
who lived at your house for a year
I weep
I take back my pillow
Skillie lies on the foot of my bed
letting me stroke her belly
one by one
I think of all
I have left

Invisible gifts
which never
leave

III

I eat plums
and tears to help me
wake from this sleep
I am in

This we said was our life
a moving picture
of a moving river

It was early morning
when the rain began
as if it were a time for dancing
where we could at the count of three

Remember sometimes how we danced
by a streetlamp in cold wind
when autumn caught our heels,
and trees were festooned with sparkling lights
on a riverbank
our feet covered with mud

and when we had danced half the night
telling our story
only to lose our place or forget the key
it was so terribly late

too late for more

Almost Dawn

Venus and the crescent moon

hover together over the hillside

their edges blurred and furry

as morning mist evaporates

i wonder

is it in the sky

or in my eye

that brief moment togetherness

sun chasing

a father

after lovers eloping

receding again behind clouds

hiding their sky dance

it will be months until

they are together again

ALICE AND THE CHESHIRE CAT

Possibly she stares at him
red hair streaming
down her back
red buttons on yellow

Possibly her eyes flash
how dare you
hands folded
in her lap

He is as stern as single malt whiskey
his eyes look deeply
out into the landscape
hanging houseplants
retired spectacles
horseshoes driftwood sculptures

Possibly she notices
his tailored suit
facing west
sleet falling

And he is kinder than she
his gaze steady yet soft
his scent lingers
eyes moving
left to right

She turns slightly
letting him in
Possibly she notices
his paw moving toward her

TELEGRAPH HILL

We used to go up on the roof
watch the fog roll in
a filmy tendril snaking its way
under the Golden Gate Bridge
one minute it is clear
next we are engulfed
in thick opaque wetness
even Coit Tower disappears

I move in close
snuggle into him
this man who is my lover
resting long locks
on his knobby shoulder
we slip into this murky stew
as evening turns to night
street lights   a blur of gold

taking in silent dank gulps
I feel my thirst

ARRIVAL

You strode into my life
   not on horseback
      nor in heavy boots

You landed
   on my breath
      whispered into my exhale

I inhaled your yearning
   the pain that brought you here

We inhale each other
   greedy for whatever
      whatever fleeting time
         there is

Your arms encircle
   a cocoon, your soft touch a caress
      you hold on   don't let go
         I could feel safe
            or trapped

Thunder talks across the meadow
   its light tap tapping
      bringing rain

Sky Ice Blue

i feel your staccato
down from
lips to breast
navel to thigh
losing its way

we are broken
embarrassed   seething
we shrink from the citadel
which beckons
as if it were meant for loss

we lose our way here amid
monotony and boredom
invisible habits
waning
we are worn thin
in steely light

when i turn to meet you
you begin to disappear
         as if walking into mist
              you lie invisible
                   buried

your song
         cryptic
                   unheard

INTERLUDE

I

There is a poem
written four ways
each distinct
in style or stanza
lengua or words
one in rhyme and the others not
each is the same poem and each is different

We are the poem
as it is written
and as it writes us
we are the walkers and the seers
we are the pawns and the princes
light streams over us
is it moonlight or a fallen star
we are the wind that blows through us
and the silken sails

We have never been before
will never be again as we are
the knots undone
i try to decipher the words of this poem
they slip away
the picture of the medina in Marrakesh
in this room
the ground for this moment
it holds a past

et tú EsteVa
a dónde vas

II

As it is written
there is a poem
in this room the picture
medina in Marrakesh
it holds a past
when i search the words
they slip away

there is a poem
words *lengua* stanza
slip away   knots undone
we hold the ground
for this moment
as it holds the past
we have never been before
and will never be again
as we are

as it is written
we are the poem
we are the sails
the winds that blow through us
the words that slip away
the light that shines on us

the poem writes itself four ways
one word by one word
each is the same
and each is different
as it writes us
we are seer and prophet
pawn and priest

walking in columns of words
i try to decipher
they slip away not stolen
but disappeared as they recede into the page

III

There is a poem it holds a past
Written one word by one word
lengua stanza lines are blurred
as it writes us etched in glass
we slip away our words unmasked
to feel the wind its murmur heard
the sighing moonlight undeterred
it writes us ship sail jib and mast

We are the dancers in the night
pawn and prophet prince and seer
illusions in blazing starlight
fleeting brilliant startled clear
we make our footsteps left then right
before our imprints disappear

IV

y tú mi amor
A dónde vas

It holds a past
the ground for this moment
in this room
the picture of the medina in Marrakesh
they slip away
(as) i try to decipher the words of this poem
the knots undone
will never be again as we are
(and) we have never been before

We are the wind that blows through us
and the silken sails
is it moonlight or a falling star
the light that streams over us
we are the pawns and the princes
we are the walkers and the seers
and as it writes us
we are the poem
as it is written

each is the same poem and each is different
one in rhyme and the others not
lengua or words
a different style or stanza
each slightly different
it is written four ways
this is a poem

CONCIERTO

Toca me
toca me
tus canciones
flotan al cielo
como las gaviotas

que remontan a las nieblas
que bailan
con la música
que suspiran como yo
cuándo yo te siento cerca de me

toca me con tú sueno

CONCERTO

Touch me
touch me
your songs
float to the sky
like the gulls

who rise into the clouds
who dance
with the music
that whispers as I do
when I feel you near

touch me with your dreams

EVE

she walks

into

him

his hands

falling leaves

weaving blue

behind her

she melts

feels his touch

ephemeral

beyond time

beyond imagination

beyond the veil

COMPLETION

The stars hold their voice
as I have held mine
I live inside skin
near the well

After love
my heart splayed open
disarmed
who am I to judge
this urgency
to give and give
and give
and want
want everything
feel everything
everything
till my last breath

Oasis

Musk at your pulse
mist on lemons
fading sun
full of day's end
jasmine in a trellised garden
a prodigal wind embracing
the ghost full of you

my heart is the white street
the muezzins call to prayer
after love the surf moon
and turquoise apron
cleanse us
as surely as the sea

at times I stroll
soothing you
in tattered Arabic and French
in a Roman villa
before rain
i am one
with your sleep
your perfume

now moonlight
caresses you

WHAT IS LEFT

Elsewhere

Is it not sheer arrogance

the dance of anger

that you crush my petals

as they open like a lotus before you

The verbal blitzkrieg that descends

no counter to contain it

petals trampled

how will I dare to bloom again

And you with your verbiage

it is your perennial cloak

bedfellow for too long

you are always right

WHAT IS LEFT

ropes of kelp draped

over driftwood

man o war

abandoned

on the sand

crumpled gull

broken coral

blue glass

rain drizzle

receding tide

my residence

in your domain

everything

i left

sharp slaps

that drove me

under

broken

a wreckage

a marriage

the seal

bloated

carrion

for the vulture

EVERY WINTER

the old comforter billows
out of the trunk
a work of the love
you never spoke aloud
nor showed
by touch

hand-stitched king-sized
it lost its tattered Indian bedspread cover
last year
but not its loft

it moves in on me
on my bed
every winter
its softness
so unlike you
your tongue a knife
lopping angry
indiscriminate
the critic in you
would never admit
it was love
plied into
soft down

warm and light
it nearly floats
above the bed
your smell long gone
its new flower print cover hiding your stitches

you must have put all your softness into it
        it is the one thing i can keep
                remember
                        you loved me
                                once

"FISHIE"
for Alexander

do you remember

breakfast

a boardwalk café

pools of water under us open

fish and plants

one minute

he was there

pointing

looking in

the next vanished

the last thing he said

 "fishie"

fifteen months old

I found him there

under the boardwalk

floating away

peaceful-like

face down

beyond my reach

you, with your long arms

grabbed his foot

pulled him out

saved his life

saved us

GOODBYE
GIVEN ALL I COULD

LEAVING I

I wander through the house
paint splotches on walls
fill my cup with orange tea

I look at leaves on sheets
stare absently at left over blue

I fell to loving
when you came to me
held my trembling waist
caressed my throat
in and out
since then you have
followed me

Flesh forgotten
we touch'd fingertips
hearts shudder
you fell in at my side
of the mirror
I wandered in and out

When you walked back
into my life
I almost didn't notice

Leaving II

Fragrant
day lily
pink
loud orange
center
trumpet majestic
I
wonder
what
I
will
say to
you
tonight

Sorry
goodbye
given
all I could
under
the circumstances

LEAVING III

Turned inside out

that place raw and open

where a piece of me is torn away

the oyster split from its safe haven

the abalone stripped from its home

crushed velvet silken and raw

turned inside out

this heart in pieces feeling

this leaving of you

how it is

I had forgotten

LEAVING IV

a single snowflake
brushes the top of her left cheek
his knee blends into hers
as she into earth
gunshots, a dog's bark
a saw so distant
sounds she would not hear
if she were moving
or if it was not so still

a hair flutters the tip of her nose
a subtle breeze
now frozen damp
on her face
she senses the difference
between herself and air
snow embracing them
as they sink into earth

she does not know yet
that one April he will be gone
that she will wish him well
that she will think of him
when clouds turn fire opal at dawn

Leaving V

I left you behind dark glasses
found dark blue glass beads
a leather thong
and eagle pendant
circling my neck
so many lifetimes ago

Reeling at the smell of musk and sunset
once it choked my senses
scrambled apostrophes
milk turned sour

I take stock of broken pieces
as they lie
feathers angled
a pile of reflections
If the moon opens a window
they fly scattered

I will give the pieces to sons
who have no memory of these shards
that forge their way
brittle and light

LEAVING VI

she showed us all
something
about the way
to go

to just sit
home
alone

in her favorite chair
so no one
could take her
anywhere
make sure
she said goodbye
and go
out like that
peaceful

who knew why
she didn't
answer her door
anymore
when they knocked
and knocked

DIVING IN

AFTER RUMI

I would not do this but for the love of it

singing my heart out until the light of dawn

the swallow's lament pierces the summer night

even the sorrow in my heart plucks the heartstrings of
my joy

why else would I go

on loving

GLASTONBURY

Beneath the Tor
I walk
checking for your reflection
in the chalice well
invoking your name
again again
sending the plume above the tin roof

nothing is softer than autumn sky
ancient roman roads
ways of druid
ways of pilgrim

I see from below
the hidden connection to place
what is lost

under   ground
the whisper   your whisper

I look into the well

emerging
you slither
out of water
trembling
slippery with oil

PERHAPS

we are all in disguise
timeless in the long dark nights of winter
maybe we   will find buckets
full of moonlight
letting in the rhythm of light
the sun is returning
maybe we all wander in concentric circles
open windows in a world of multiple truths

perhaps every stone has its moment
what's happening now
is a replay
not mine not yours,
maybe we all drift
I am an outsider
swinging back and forth
on a shoestring

we are all in disguise
in concentric circles
timeless in the long dark nights
of winter

PETALS OF MORNING

fragments of memory
rags of the past
a collage on the wings of the moon
scraps of cedar
droppings of forget-me-nots
and ghosts of yesterday
walk in procession
wandering in and out of thought forms
masked mirrored or verbatim

i carry the winnowed grains
of a hundred lifetimes in my heart
present in this moment of uncertainty

stepping out into the unknown
the invisible traveler
upends static versions of reality

exposing what is

In the Shrine Room

Eruption of sound
tumult of pillows   blankets
preparing to sit

The surrealist
melts watches daggers rainbows
sitting   melts   my heart

Outside bees buzzing
chant wisdom meditation
now   I am weeping

Mauve dusk surrenders
bittersweet comes the darknesss
suddenly   regret

To be tethered to
the mystery of this life
is   enough   water

On Retreat

I

Mists sweep off mountains
from the west
into the well of the valley
laying over it inch by inch
foot by foot
until we are enveloped

we slip in and out
of fog
in our minds
opening long-closed portals
to inner vortices and buried pain
laying down taproots
to our ancestral home

bridling my mare
we track west
diving into darkness
the unknowable
relentless our journey unfolds

II

we walk step by measured step
one foot
in front
of the other
catch my breath
heel to toe rolling up
breathe in
heel to toe rolling down
breathe out
i hear the squeak of a swing
and my shoe

our luminous world

the wind our sail

water our boat

earth our anchor

fire   the flame in our hearts

III

I feel you snow as you whisper
come out, come out
I am falling, falling
As you fall into yourself
come, sit with me
stand with me
walk with me

We are not alone you and I
there are others
seen and unseen
who hear my whisper
insistent serene
you'll need bring nothing more
than your Heart

I won't keep it
only for this moment
while we sit together
sway together
here in the solace of my arms

IV

Every day storm clouds come
dark thunder wind
every day we pray for rain
today a few drops
over the hill
a fire still
burning

we pray for sunrise
for the kestrel's low hover in the meadow
we pray for
the wild pleasure of red poppies

my windows are open
morning has taken off her shirt
the barn swallow in his finery
midnight rust and amber
sits on my shoulder
asking directions
clouds answer tomorrow
the wind whispers now

V

Nothing Happens   (Next)

I've lived in the hall of mirrors

Timeless

Everywhere my reflection

In the temple of this body

I   disappear

ONCE A TREE

I saw her
where she stood
looking south
at the foot
of the golden cliff
which rose
perpendicular
above the beach

Her shawl
an off-white shroud
of serpentine gauze
clung to her body
swaying in late afternoon
I can't say
exactly
from where
she came
draped in the style
of ancient Greece
Mesopotamia
or India

She gestured
toward the south
without moving
I turned to look
followed her gaze
into the distance
beyond where
I could see

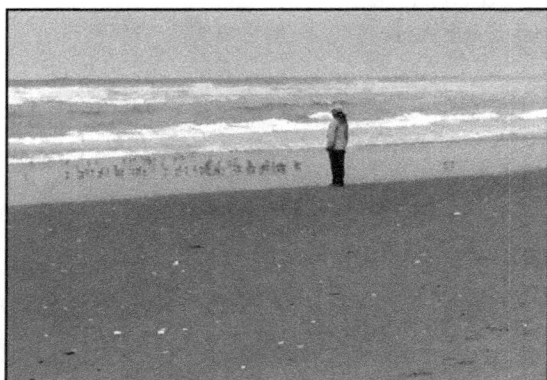

MURMURATION

In memory of Carol 1945 - 2019

She walks along the nearly flat beach
water swirling round her feet as waves
wash in wash out
sanderlings
hundreds of them rushing
little feet scampering
in S curves back and forth
like the waves
with whom
they dance
with waves
they run
one grand
unison scurry
as waves recede
a swift poke into the sand
captures a ghost shrimp
at the bottom of bubbles
created by receding waves
they scurry again,
swirl back and forth
undulating ribbons

she moves
among them rapt
white baseball cap
turquoise coat
slowly stops
pensive

a flash of gray
a sudden leap
skyward
they fly
as
one

VOYAGE: THE BODY WITHOUT LIGHTS OR MUSIC

hand over hand
thirty feet of stone
I was here before
and now
I am here again
living on clouds
and frozen water

I am a streak of light in the sky
sunset
to the tune of no clouds
to breathe like a fairy
once I asked for this

the breeze shimmers
juices run wildly
I should have never
locked the door

moon conjunct venus
rose clouds
once I asked
to see the world
through your eyes
forces of wind ice water
pushing at the shore
cacophony
of a hundred geese

when she turned
stunned
she was an eagle
to follow
as far as my eyes
the sound of ice

once I asked
for this

where I was
before
the blue flame in my heart
the mum's startle
her voice followed me
backward
over old ground
without dandelions

and I am looking at
snow falling
the shadow palace dissolves
layers of winter

it is time to shed
my dark navy
once I asked for this

FINAL NOTES

GRATITUDE

There are so many to thank for making this volume
possible—mentors, fellow writers, patients who shared
their stories, good friends, my children, my parents, and
spiritual teachers who always had faith in me. Without
all of you, I would not have had the confidence and
determination needed to allow these poems to see the
light I hope they deserve. I am full of gratitude to you all.
Specifically I thank mentors Max Regan, John Latham,
and Jack Collom for inspiring, encouraging, and helping
me hone this work. I also thank two physicians, now
deceased: Isabelle Biddlle DO and Gurth Carpenter
MD, who mentored me and generously shared what it
means to be a real healer. I thank the spiritual teachers
who inspired me: Terry Ray, Neil McKinley, and
Norman Elizondo.

For my writing friends who supported me, especially
those in my writing group (you know who you are), I am
so appreciative. I thank Laura Marshall and Lisa Birman
for help in creating the manuscript and its art. I thank
Ed and Deb Shapiro, Nin, Lorene, Kathleen, David
Rome, Jennifer Heath, and my sister Lois for all kinds
of good advice. Lastly, I am so grateful to Pat Flores and
Elizabeth Upper for helping me get the Spanish right.

To my children, for your continued love and support
despite the rigorous and demanding schedule you had
to live through during my working years as a physician, I
cannot thank you enough.

Who is Julie?

Julie and I first met when I was 16 and she was 18. She was Juliet Aroian then. She had wanted to be a physician since she was five. She went to Stanford and graduated in 1964, having spent a year in Europe—six months at Stanford-in-Italy, and another six months hitchhiking all over Europe with my brother, whom she later married. Medical school at NYU followed, then internship and residency. The challenges of her medical training polished her like a gemstone, and she developed into a wise and intuitive physician.

She settled in Colorado and opened her solo private practice as a family doctor in 1973 when her first son was a year old. She loved her work and her patients. She loved delivering babies and experiencing the sacred wind that comes through the open door at birth and death. She savored being in the presence of all that life, death, illness, and health presented to her. She first began writing poetry in the late 1980s, when poems just came to her, and in the early 1990s she began studying the poet's craft with Max Regan, and later with Jack Collom and John Latham.

Julie loves to travel, and has travelled the world extensively both for pleasure and for work. She has visited Europe, Morocco, India, Kenya, Peru, Mexico, Nicaragua, and Tibet. She has done volunteer work in Haiti, and most extensively in Tibet, where she spent a total of nearly seven months (in three separate trips) working for the Surmang Foundation. There she helped train two young physicians to deliver outstanding medical care in a rural area where there was previously no care and no running water, electricity, sanitation, or modern conveniences like stores, mail, or public transportation. Their work has transformed the health of the local people.

The natural world nourishes Julie, and she loves to be in nature and explore new places. She is an avid gardener, and lives in the mountains where she can watch clouds all day. She retired from her medical practice in 2013 and spends as much time outdoors as she can.

Over the years, I have seen the qualities that I loved about her when first we met develop into great gifts - the brightness has become brilliance, her ability to engage and connect with people has become deep empathy and compassion, and her rare qualities of openness have engendered a creative receptivity that finds voice in these poems, a gift from her soul to the heart and soul of her readers.

Lorene Mills is a veteran journalist and interview host (for Report from Santa Fe) in New Mexico on KANW. In 2019 she was named a Santa Fe Living Treasure, and was awarded the Best in Government Award by Common Cause for her work in ethics reform.

About Baksun Books & Arts

The mission of Baksun Books & Arts (fiscally sponsored by the Boulder County Arts Alliance) is to produce imaginative projects, publish books of poetry and prose, and curate art exhibitions (frequently on behalf of social and environmental justice), accompanied by comprehensive exhibition catalogues.

Baksun attempts to approach and examine issues from as many creative and interactive angles as possible in the firm conviction that the arts can influence lasting change.

Baksun was founded by Jennifer Heath in 1992 as a small press dedicated to de-commodifying the word and, in 1994, began creating educational and topical art exhibitions as well. It has reached thousands, of all ages, through diverse activities in museums, galleries, grassroots organizations, neighborhoods, schools, children's groups, libraries, and the Internet.

Baksun is dedicated to bringing together strategies for confronting today's issues, illustrating and contextualizing them to highlight the beauty of our natural and cultural gifts and resources, and to heal. The arts not only "speak truth to power," but uphold that truth and carry it forward.

Selected Recent Baksun Publications

❖ *The Last Tourist in Bali*, by Tree Bernstein, 2020

❖ *Murmurations: Wingèd Beings Sacred and Profane*, exhibition catalogue, 2019

❖ *Imaginary Maps: Expeditions to Uncover Aprocryphal, Unsubstantiated and Forbidden Places*, exhibition catalogue, 2018

❖ *How I learned to Cook: An Artist's Life*, by Barbara Shark, 2018

❖ *Addled Smoke Material: Collaborative Poems 1972-2017*, by Jack Collom and Reed Bye, 2017

❖ *Celebration! A History of the Visual Arts in Boulder*, exhibition catalogue, 2016

❖ *"The Map is Not the Territory": Parallel Paths— Palestinians, Native Americans, Irish*, exhibition catalogue, 2015

❖ *Water Water Everywhere: Paean to a Vanishing Resource*, exhibition catalogue, 2014

BAKSUN BOOKS
1838 PINE STREET,
BOULDER, CO 80302 USA

www.ingramcontent.com/pod-product-compliance
Lightning Source LLC
Chambersburg PA
CBHW020550030426
42337CB00013B/1039